The Chinook People

by Pamela Ross

Consultant:
Gary Johnson, Chinook Cultural Officer
The Chinook Tribe

Bridgestone Books
an imprint of Capstone Press
Mankato, Minnesota

Bridgestone Books are published by Capstone Press
818 North Willow Street, Mankato, Minnesota 56001
http://www.capstone-press.com

Library of Congress Cataloging-in-Publication Data
Ross, Pamela, 1962–
    The Chinook people/by Pamela Ross.
    p. cm. — (Native peoples)
    Includes bibliographical references and index.
    Summary: Provides an overview of the past and present lives of the Chinook people,
covering their daily activities, customs, family life, religion, government, history, and
interaction with the United States government.
    ISBN 0-7368-0076-X
    1. Chinook Indians—History—Juvenile literature. 2. Chinook Indians—Social life and
customs—Juvenile literature. [1. Chinook Indians. 2. Indians of North America—Northwest,
Pacific.] I. Title. II. Series.
E99.C57R67 1999
973'.049741—dc21

                                                              98-18424
                                                                 CIP
                                                                 AC

Editorial Credits
Timothy W. Larson, editor; Timothy Halldin, cover designer and illustrator;
    Sheri Gosewisch, photo researcher
Photo Credits
Aigrette Photography/Brenda Moseley, cover, 6, 10, 14, 16; Marilyn Moseley LaMantia,
    12, 20
The Chinook Tribe/Linda Dombrowski, 8, 18

Table of Contents

Map 4
Fast Facts 5

The Chinook People 7
Homes, Food, and Clothing 9
The Chinook Family 11
Chinook Potlatches 13
Chinook Religion 15
Chinook Government 17
Chinook History 19
Creation Story 21

Hands on: Play Fish-Trap Tag 22
Words to Know 23
Read More 23
Useful Addresses 24
Internet Sites 24
Index 24

Map

Canada

Washington

Oregon

United States

Mexico

Traditional Location

Fast Facts

Today, many Chinook people live in communities on lands called reservations. Many Chinook people live like other North Americans. But they also work to save the traditions of the past. They do not want Chinook ways, values, and language to be forgotten. These facts show some Chinook ways of the past.

Homes: The Chinook built long, rectangle-shaped houses. They built their homes with cedar boards.

Food: The Chinook were fishers and hunters. Salmon fish was their most important food. They ate meat from elk, deer, bears, and whales. The Chinook also gathered wild potatoes and berries.

Clothing: The Chinook wore clothing they made from cedar bark or leather. Some of this clothing included shirts, leggings, and skirts. The Chinook also wore hats. Women made the hats with cedar strips and bear grass.

Language: The Chinook spoke the Chinookan language. They also created Chinook jargon. People used this language when trading goods.

Traditional Location: The northwest coast of the United States is the Chinook's traditional location. Most Chinook lived in what are now Oregon and Washington. Many Chinook still live in their traditional homeland.

The Chinook People

The Chinook people have lived in the Pacific Northwest for thousands of years. Most Chinook have lived in what are now Oregon and Washington. Many still live there today.

In the past, many Chinook villages were near the Columbia River. Other Chinook villages were along Willapa Bay.

Water was important to the Chinook people. They fished on the Pacific Ocean, Willapa Bay, and the Columbia River. They used large canoes to travel and trade on these waters.

The Chinook people were excellent traders. They traded among themselves and with other Native Americans. Later, they traded with Europeans who came to the area. The Chinook traded goods such as fish, canoes, and blankets.

Today, most Chinook live like other North Americans. Some live on land called reservations. Many Chinook people still value traditional ways.

Many Chinook people still value traditional ways.

Homes, Food, and Clothing

In the past, the Chinook people built longhouses. Longhouses were long, rectangle-shaped homes. Fifty or more people often lived in each house.

The Chinook people built their longhouses out of cedar boards. Each house had benches, beds, and fire pits. Some Chinook families carved wooden house poles for their homes. Carve means to shape wood by cutting it. The house poles showed the histories of the families.

The Chinook people did not need to farm the land. Men caught salmon. They sometimes hunted whales on the ocean. Men also hunted elk, deer, and bears. Women gathered wild potatoes and berries.

The Chinook wore clothing they made from cedar bark or leather. They made skirts, robes, and hats from cedar bark. They made shirts and leggings from leather.

Salmon is still an important part of the Chinook diet.

The Chinook Family

Family has always been important to the Chinook people. Chinook families lived together in longhouses. As many as 100 members of the same family lived together. There were children, fathers, mothers, and grandparents. Aunts, uncles, and cousins also lived in the longhouses.

Groups of Chinook families lived together in large villages. More than 1,000 Chinook people often lived in one village.

Family members helped raise children. Men taught boys how to use canoes. Men also showed boys how to hunt, fish, and make tools.

Women showed girls how to trade goods. Women also showed girls how to gather, prepare, and store food.

Grandparents taught children the history and traditions of the Chinook people. They shared many traditions through stories.

Family has always been important to the Chinook.

Chinook Potlatches

Chinook families held potlatches to show their wealth. A potlatch is a special gathering with a feast and gift-giving. Families also hosted potlatches to share their wealth with others. Wealthy Chinook families often hosted large potlatches.

Families often held potlatches to mark important family events. These events included weddings and births.

Potlatches often were grand events. They could last several days. Hundreds of guests would attend. People ate, drank, and told stories. All guests received gifts from the hosts.

Potlatches were important to the Chinook. Families might take months or years to prepare for potlatches. Today, Chinook families still have potlatches.

All guests at Chinook potlatches receive gifts.

Chinook Religion

The Chinook people had their own religion. They followed a set of spiritual beliefs. The Chinook religion said all things in nature had spirits. The spirits provided everything the Chinook needed to live.

The Chinook religion taught Chinook people to respect nature. They did not take more than they needed. The Chinook gave thanks to the spirits. They gave thanks for the food, clothing, and shelter nature provided.

Today, some Chinook people practice the traditional Chinook religion. Others follow Christianity. Christianity is a religion based on the teachings of Jesus Christ. Some Chinook people follow the Indian Shaker religion. This religion combines the Chinook religion and Christianity.

Some Chinook people practice the Chinook religion.

Chinook Government

Each Chinook village had a leader. A leader could be a man or a woman. A leader's first son or daughter often became the next leader.

Leaders met with villagers to make important decisions about village life. They made group decisions about government and business. Leaders from each village sometimes met. They would meet to talk about matters facing all Chinook people.

Today, the Chinook people have a tribal council. Nine people make up the Chinook tribal council. The Chinook people vote for each of these leaders.

The U.S. government does not recognize the Chinook government. Recognize means to accept as official. The Chinook people are working hard to be recognized.

The Chinook people have a tribal council.

Chinook History

The Chinook came to the Pacific Northwest thousands of years ago. Over time, the Chinook became powerful. They had their own government. They created their own systems of money and trade. The Chinook also had their own religion, art, and music.

The Chinook way of life started changing in the 1700s. Explorers came to the Chinook homeland. Many others followed. Settlers soon moved to the area. They claimed Chinook lands. They set up their own governments.

During the 1800s, sickness killed many Chinook people. The U.S. government took Chinook land. The Chinook homeland became part of the United States.

Today, there are more than 2,000 Chinook people. They are working with other Native Americans to receive government recognition.

Today, the Chinook are working with other Native Americans for government recognition.

Creation Story

In the past, the Chinook told important stories. The stories often explained history, traditions, and nature. The Chinook once told this story to explain how they began.

Long ago, Old Man South Wind traveled north. He traveled up the Pacific Coast. He was very hungry. He met a giant named Old Woman. He asked Old Woman for food. Old Woman gave him a net to catch fish.

Old Man South Wind caught a whale from the ocean. Old Woman said not to cut the whale across its back. Old Man South Wind did not listen. He cut the whale across its back. The whale turned into a bird named Thunderbird.

Thunderbird flew to the top of Saddleback Mountain. The bird laid eggs in a nest. Old Woman found the eggs. She pushed the eggs out of the nest and down the mountain. The Chinook people came out of the eggs.

Thunderbird flew to the top of Saddleback Mountain.

Hands on: Play Fish-Trap Tag

The Chinook had 17 ways to catch fish. Sometimes they used traps. But fishing with traps was not always easy. The Chinook had to set their traps carefully to catch fish. Fish-trap tag shows how hard Chinook fishing could be.

What You Need

A group of seven to 11 players

What You Do

1. Choose one player to be the fish. Divide the other players into two groups. These players are the fishers.
2. Each group of fishers joins hands. This forms two fish traps. Fishers must keep their hands joined during the game.
3. Have the fish run away from the fishers. Give the fish a short head start.
4. Have the fishers try to circle and catch the fish in their trap.
5. The fish can try to break through the trap.
6. Choose a new fish once a group of fishers catches the fish.

Words to Know

council (KOUN-suhl)—a group of leaders
potlatch (POT-lach)—a special gathering with a feast and gift-giving
recognize (REK-uhg-nize)—to accept as official
religion (ri-LIJ-uhn)—a set of spiritual beliefs people follow
traditional (truh-DISH-uhn-uhl)—having to do with the ways of the past

Read More

Liptak, Karen. *Indians of the Pacific Northwest.* New York: Facts on File, 1991.

Press, Petra. *Indians of the Northwest: Traditions, History, Legends, and Life.* Philadelphia: Courage Books, 1997.

Sherrow, Victoria. *American Indian Children of the Past.* Brookfield, Conn.: Millbrook Press, 1997.

Trafzer, Clifford E. *The Chinook.* New York: Chelsea House Publishers, 1990.

Useful Addresses

Chinook Tribal Office
P.O. Box 228
Chinook, WA 98614

**Small Tribes Organization
of Western Washington**
3040 96th Street South
Tacoma, WA 98587

Internet Sites

Chinook Jargon—About Chinook
http://www.corp.direct.ca/ironmtn/chinook/about.html

Discover Cathlapotle! Chinook Indian Country
http://www-adm.pdx.edu/user/anth/cathla/country.htm

Northwest Native Americans
http://www.germantown.k12.il.us/html/northwest.html

Index

clothing, 9, 15

Columbia River, 7

family, 11, 13

food, 9, 11, 15, 21

longhouse, 9, 11

potlatch, 13

religion, 15, 19

Saddleback Mountain, 21

salmon, 9

settlers, 19

tribal council, 17

Willapa Bay, 7